Boldmere School

PARENT TEACHER ASSOCIATION Prize

Presented to

IAN HOLMES

1982

ADVANCED MOTORCYCLING

Geoff
Carless

EP PUBLISHING LIMITED

Published by EP Publishing Limited, Bradford Road, East Ardsley, Wakefield, West Yorkshire

ISBN 0 7158 0776 5

First published 1982

ACKNOWLEDGEMENTS

The author and publishers are grateful to the following for their help in the preparation of this book:

Kawasaki UK Ltd., Deal Avenue, Trading Estate, Slough, Bucks.
Belstaff International Ltd., Caroline Street, Longton, Stoke-on-Trent, Staffs.
Robert Saluz, Upton, Poole, Dorset.
Dick Ganderton, Verwood, Dorset.
Motorcycling, Westover House, West Quay Road, Poole, Dorset.
Griffin Helmets Ltd., Highfield Road, Cradley, Halesowen, West Midlands.
Rivetts Leathers Ltd., 234 High Road, Leytonstone, London E11.
Lewis Leathers Ltd., 124 Great Portland Street, London W1.
Pentax UK Ltd., Pentax House, South Hill Avenue, South Harrow, Middlesex.

Cover illustration by Arthur Saluz. Other illustrations by Tony Gardiner and Arthur Saluz.

Text set in 11/13 point Melior, printed in Great Britain by photolithography by G. Beard & Son Ltd, Brighton, Sussex, and bound by Seawhite Ltd, Brighton, Sussex.

CONTENTS

THE AUTHOR

Geoff Carless was born in Solihull in 1949 and developed an interest in motorcycles almost from that date. Both his father and grandfather owned motorcycle combinations, and sitting in the sidecar was his main means of travel.

Before leaving school Geoff passed the Cycling Proficiency Test, after deciding that road safety was an important factor in staying alive. He bought his first motorcycle as soon as he was old enough legally to ride on the road and has rarely been without one ever since.

In 1971 Geoff Carless joined the Police with the sole ambition of becoming a Traffic Patrol Motorcyclist. After passing both the Advanced Motorcycle and Advanced Car Driving courses to Grade 1 standard he joined the Traffic Department serving two years on the bikes and one year on Motorway Patrol duty.

In 1977 he became a motorcycle journalist, joining the staff of *Motorcycling*. He has written numerous articles on the subject of safety, and is also employed as the Technical Consultant on the Daily Mail Motorcycle Show Review.

In 1979 his first book, *Motorcycling for Beginners*, was published, and this book is a follow-up to that success.

INTRODUCTION

In my first book, *Motorcycling for Beginners*, I explained all the basic techniques of riding a motorcycle. It was a book designed for the complete novice, although it did include a section on motorway riding, which is not part of the standard test but is an important part of modern travel.

Advanced Motorcycling is designed to help riders further these basic techniques and develop their skills. Passing a test is only the start. All it does is change the details on your driving licence; it does not make you a motorcyclist. A sound basic knowledge must be accompanied by plenty of practice and experience. Keep learning.

Advanced Motorcycling is a natural progression for the motorcyclist. It is not, as the name may suggest to some people, all about exceeding speed limits, but about professional, planned, safe riding. It will alert you to the dangers that exist and detail how to minimise the risk of an accident.

Police motorcyclists receive excellent training

I was trained by one of Britain's Police Forces, and became a member of the most respected body of motorcyclists in the world. If I can pass on some of my training, knowledge and experience in an effort to help road safety I am happy.

I would just ask that you bear one thing in mind; I am still learning. I am adapting my riding techniques to match the changing road and traffic conditions. Nobody knows it all.

Geoff Carless

THE MOTORCYCLE

Motorcycles not only vary greatly in engine capacity and power output, but also in their design for use. There are sports bikes, touring bikes, trail bikes and commuters.

Sports machines, or so-called 'sports machines', start at about 100cc and range through to 1300cc. They vary in power and performance, with the larger models being capable of exceeding 130mph and producing 120bhp. Some bikes in this category are often used as touring machines, although this has the disadvantage of thirsty fuel consumption.

Two of the larger sports motorcycles, capable of 135mph or more

Powerful 1000cc tourer with high-rise
handlebars and windscreen,
and additional foglamps

Touring motorcycles are generally designed with a less power-ful, more economical engine. The riding position is more relaxed and the seat a lot softer for greater comfort on long journeys. It is generally accepted that touring bikes have a large engine capacity; usually of 500cc and above, although some smaller bikes lend themselves quite well to the task.

250cc tourer

Trail bikes are dual purpose motorcycles, capable of being used on the road or on the rough. They range from 50cc to 800cc, are equipped with dual-purpose tyres, and have gear ratios that are a compromise between road and off-road use.

175cc trail bike

800cc trail bike capable of over 100mph

Every motorcycle can come into the category of 'commuter'. Sports bikes, touring bikes and trail bikes are all used to transport their owners to and from work. There are, however, specific small capacity motorcycles that are designed and marketed as 'commuters'. They are lightweights in the 50cc to 250cc range that are economical, easy to ride and maintain, and ideal for short trips along busy roads.

The choice of motorcycle is always a personal one, but certain factors must be taken into account. Initial cost, running cost, insurance, weight, seat height, etc., are all considerations to be made. It is pointless, and dangerous, for a short person to buy a bike with a seat height designed for a tall person, which makes it impossible to reach the ground in order to support the machine. It is a waste of money, both initially and because of running costs, to buy a 1300cc superbike just to travel a few miles to and from work. And so it goes on.

Think before buying. Check all the necessary details you can, and read any relevant road tests that have been published in motorcycle magazines and papers. You don't need a big powerful motorcycle to practice advanced riding techniques; the skill of the rider is more important than the machine he rides.

1300cc tourer

The choice between two-stroke and four-stroke is also a personal one. Two-stroke engines run on a mixture of petrol and oil, usually have a peaky or fairly narrow power band, and have little or no engine braking.

Four-stroke engines are becoming more popular, with exhaust emission controls getting tougher, and are slowly pushing two-strokes into the background. They offer a very wide spread of power, better torque and better fuel consumption.

Four-stroke engine

1. As the piston descends it creates a vacuum in the cylinder which draws in the fuel/air mix through the inlet valve.
2. As the piston starts to rise both the inlet and exhaust valves are closed causing the mixture to be compressed.
3. The spark plug ignites the mixture and the force from the explosion pushes the piston down.
4. As the piston moves up on stroke three the exhaust valve is open allowing the burnt gases to be pushed out.
5. The cycle starts again using the exhaust valve for a fraction of a second to help draw in the mixture.

NOTE: the valves are opened and closed by either rocker arms or camshafts which are driven by pushrods or a chain directly from the crankshaft.

  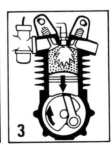 

Two-stroke engine

1. As the piston rises it compresses the mixture in the chamber, and draws more into the partial vacuum in the crankcases. The piston itself operates the inlet and exhaust ports.
2. At around top dead centre the spark plug ignites the mixture and the explosion forces the piston down, at the same time compressing the mixture in the crankcases.
3. Just after the piston passes the exhaust port it opens other ports which allows the fresh mixture under pressure to find its way from the crankcases to the compression chamber, and the cycle starts again.

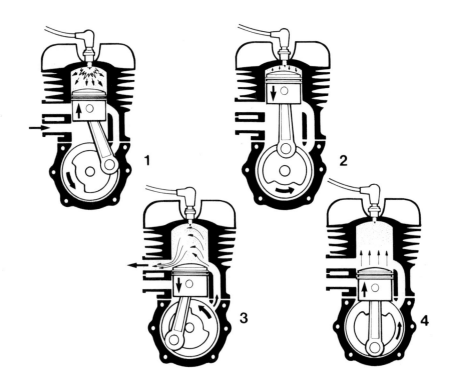

THE RIDER

Concentration

Concentration is defined as the complete application of mind and body to a particular endeavour, and the exclusion of everything not connected with that endeavour.

Today's road and traffic conditions demand that all motorcyclists exercise full concentration every time they venture on to the road. Motorists can get away with a slight lack of concentration, usually resulting in nothing more than a slightly dented car. Motorcyclists do not have a protective box around them, and only have two wheels to balance on. Lack of concentration may result in an accident that can not only damage the bike, but also injure the rider.

Concentration not only helps to avoid accidents but also aids anticipation. Thinking ahead and planning every move is the basis of advanced riding, and you can't think ahead if your riding does not have your full application.

Expert and smooth handling and operation of the motorcycle also requires full concentration. Bad gear changes, late braking and fierce acceleration can all be avoided. Bad machine control, and lack of appreciation, reflect in its movements on the road.

Attitude

A rider's mental attitude is also an important factor in road safety. It is dangerous to take revenge on your frustrations by riding furiously on the road. It therefore follows that to go out riding after an argument, or after receiving bad news, is foolhardy and potentially dangerous.

Reaction Time

Reaction time is defined as the time taken between seeing the need for action and actually taking that action.

Two-thirds of a second (0.66s) is not a very long period of time. In fact it is very difficult to even imagine it. But it can be a killer. Travelling at 30mph you cover 44 feet in one second. So in two-thirds of a second you travel nearly 30 feet, approximately the width of a main road junction, between seeing the need to brake or accelerate and actually starting to brake or accelerate.

Efforts to reduce this reaction time are essential, and there are certain exercises and sports that will sharpen the reactions and reflexes, and reduce it to below half a second.

Sports like squash, badminton and table tennis are ideal, or you can ask a friend to help you with this reaction-improving exercise.

Have your friend hold a pencil at one end between his thumb and forefinger. Start by holding your thumb and forefinger just apart from the pencil near its other end. As your friend lets go you try to catch it. When you improve you will be able to move further up the pencil, giving you less chance to catch it. Be sure it is dropped at random intervals.

Physical and Mental Fitness

Keeping physically fit is essential. A healthy body builds a healthy mind. Travelling long distances is very tiring, so fitness should be aimed at producing stamina rather than strength. Running and jogging are two ideal methods of building stamina, as are squash and badminton which also help reactions and reflexes.

Mental fitness goes hand in hand with physical fitness. An alert mind goes with a healthy body. Tiredness, or the effects of a heavy cold or flu, can result in poor mental ability. Therefore, concentration is lost and reaction time can run into seconds rather than a fraction of a second.

Clothing

Helmets and visors

Not only a safety requirement, but also a legal one in this country. An approved helmet must be worn by riders and pillion passengers when the motorcycle is used on the road.

There are two basic styles, open face and full face: both are available in either glass fibre or polycarbonate.

Glass fibre helmets are slightly heavier and more expensive than those made of polycarbonate, and they have fewer drawbacks. They can be cleaned easily, painted or take stickers. Polycarbonate helmets cannot be painted or have stickers attached, and care has to be taken with cleaning. Solvents, paints and glues can weaken the plastic shell and make it completely useless.

Of the two styles the full face helmet is probably the most widely used. It offers greater protection in that the chin guard stops facial injuries. It is also warmer in cold weather.

Open face helmets are usually worn more by small bike and moped riders. They are also preferred by trail riders because they allow the rider to get more fresh air when the going gets strenuous.

Eye protection is essential, no matter which helmet is chosen. A visor is a standard fitting on full face helmets, but open face types usually only have a peak. Closing the visor on a full face helmet completes the all round protection that this style offers.

Visors for open face helmets clip on to the front of the helmet with press studs. Some can be raised, like on a full face version, but many are fixed and prone to misting.

Full face helmet

Open face helmet

Goggles are rare these days, but are still used with both open and full face helmets. Their popularity is with the trail riders, and this is reflected in the type of goggles now available. The older glass type are giving way to the plastic ski style, which can take clip-on tinted lenses and have adjustable air vents for demisting.

Goggles with tinted clip-on

Visor on full face helmet

Visor care

Proper care of visors and goggles is essential if perfect vision is to be maintained.

The following three precautions will extend the life of your visor and ensure that scratches are kept to a minimum:

1. Never wipe your visor with a glove or overmitt; any dirt particles will scratch the soft visor.
2. Wash the visor regularly by totally immersing it in warm soapy water. Rinse with clean water and allow to drip dry. Polish with a clean soft cloth.
3. Smear the inside with a small amount of washing-up liquid to avoid misting.

Remember: a scratched visor is dangerous in wet or dark conditions, and lethal in wet *and* dark conditions. Keep it clean and renew it regularly.

Leathers

Expensive but worth it, is the best way to describe a set of leathers for road use. Available as either one-piece or two-piece, or as separate jacket and jeans, a leather suit helps to keep out the cold.

Being a fairly tight fit a set of leathers also keeps the rider streamlined, with no annoying baggy clothing flapping in the wind. And the protection offered in the event of a sliding accident is far greater than nylon or waxed cotton. Leather has saved many riders from losing a lot of skin.

For general road use, and touring, a two-piece suit is probably the best buy. The jacket and trousers zip together at the waist, but can be worn separately if desired.

As with all clothing, buy the best you can afford. Look for a suit that offers extra padding to the knees, elbows, hips and shoulders, and has pockets for carrying a wallet, money, keys, etc.

Whilst a set of leathers will keep out a very light shower they are not waterproof, and an oversuit should always be carried. If they do get wet they should be dried cold – excessive heat will damage the leather.

One-piece leather suits *(left)* and two-piece *(right)*

Oversuits

One-piece, two-piece, lined, unlined, nylon, waxed-cotton, or any combination is the choice facing every buyer of an oversuit. Most serious riders have two suits; a lined one for the cold weather and an unlined one for summer wear.

A one-piece, unlined, nylon suit will fold very small and can be strapped to the seat behind the rider, using rubber aero-elastics, when not being worn. They are ideal for wearing in warm weather.

A lined, two-piece suit, either nylon or waxed-cotton, is the best buy for the colder weather. The jacket can be worn on its own and the trousers carried on the bike, or the complete suit can be worn.

For many years waxed-cotton, thorn-proof material has been the fabric for oversuits for motorcyclists who want to keep dry. Recently, however, it is losing its popularity in favour of nylon.

Whilst waxed-cotton is certainly waterproof it is also very greasy to the touch, and not suitable for wearing over light coloured clothing. Nylon, whilst not quite so waterproof, is dry and clean to the touch, and is ideal for wearing over most clothes. It is the material chosen by most commuters, and certainly by those who wear suits and white shirts.

Some nylon suits are guaranteed 100 per cent waterproof, and whilst initially these are more expensive, they do have the advantage that they can be changed if they leak. Some of these suits are rubberised and can cause the rider to become 'wet' by sweating. They are usually very warm, but suffer from a lack of ventilation.

Reflective and fluorescent jackets and belts are becoming increasing popular with the growing need to be easily seen on the the road. Some oversuits have built-in panels of brightly coloured reflective/fluorescent material which can be seen at night.

Many riders buy fluorescent belts, vests or jackets, which are designed for daylight use, and expect to be seen at night. But they can't be; night riding requires a reflective material – one that will shine in car headlights. Riders who require all round protection should buy a garment that is both fluorescent and reflective.

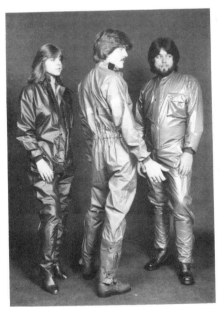

One-piece and two-piece oversuits

Underwear

During warm weather conditions normal underclothes are more than adequate, but in cold climates, and when travelling long distances, some extra protection is required.

Some of the older methods are still used in emergencies, but modern thermal underwear is now taking over.

Using a pair of ladies nylon tights may not sound very manly but it is an excellent way of keeping your legs warm. A folded newspaper inside the jacket across the chest and stomach is also a very good, and cheap, way of keeping out the cold.

Being prepared for the cold is half the problem. It's no good starting out on a long journey to suddenly find you do not have enough warm clothing. Companies like Damart sell various one- and two-piece sets of thermal underwear – a material that is designed to retain heat. It can, however, be expensive, and a cheaper alternative for shorter journeys is a long-sleeved vest and longjohns, normally available from Army surplus stores.

Gloves

Keeping hands warm and dry in cold wet weather is the curse of all motorcylists, and everything from plastic bags to rubber washing-up gloves has been used.

In warm weather gloves are still important, and a thin pair of unlined leather ones is the normal type worn.

Dolomite gloves

Leather is not waterproof, so a pair of nylon or waxed-cotton overmitts is essential, and can be carried in an oversuit pocket.

As winter starts the unlined gloves will have to give way to lined ones, together with the added protection of overmitts.

Very cold weather is best beaten by leather mitts lined with lambswool. Keeping the fingers together keeps them warmer, and the extra space allows silk, thermal or heated inner gloves to be worn. Heated gloves have small wire heating elements along the thumb, finger sections and across the back, that are powered from the bike's battery. They can be plugged in and used as and when necessary.

When buying overmitts look for a pair that have elasticated arm sections. They will form a seal over the sleeves of your oversuit and prevent water running down into the gloves.

Lined mitts – vital in winter

Heated gloves

Boots

A good pair of boots is a must for any serious rider. Riding in shoes and socks is to be discouraged at all times.

With so many different types of boot available a lot of care must be taken to select the right ones for you. Unlined, lined, leather, rubber, etc., etc.

Leather is not waterproof, so if leather boots, of whatever style, are chosen you should also buy a pair of overboots, either rubber, nylon or waxed-cotton.

Some firms are now making waterproof boots that look like leather motorcycle boots, a good example of which are the Derri boots made by the Marbot company.

If unlined boots are chosen a pair of seaboot type or thermal socks will be needed to keep warm in cold weather. Heated inner soles are also available, and work in a similar way to the gloves.

Extras

Helmet pelmet – a shaped piece of vinyl material that is fixed to the front of a full face helmet chin bar. A strip of Velcro tape is stuck to the helmet and the pelmet can be removed and replaced as necessary. It hangs down in front of the neck and keeps cold draughts from entering the helmet.

Helmet pelmet

Under-helmet – a thin balaclava made from silk or cotton and worn under the helmet. It has a slit for the eyes, and the remainder covers the face, ears and neck to keep your head warm in cold weather.

Under-helmet

THE LAW

Documents

Before a motorcycle can be used on a road in Great Britain the rider must ensure that certain documents are in his possession.

Driving licence – whether full or provisional it must be current and cover the type of vehicle(s) to be used.

If the rider is a learner he will hold a provisional licence and must also display 'L' plates to the front and rear of the motorcycle.

Insurance – every vehicle used on the road must be covered by at least third party insurance, but it is obviously better to take the best cover you can afford.

Test certificate – when a vehicle reaches three years old it has to be tested for roadworthiness, and have yearly tests thereafter.

Vehicle excise licence – vehicle road tax is renewable yearly or every six months, and requires the registration document, insurance certificate or cover note, and test certificate if applicable, to be produced at each renewal.

Speed Limits

Every road in Britain is covered by a maximum speed limit, and a few are also governed by a minimum limit as well. Most of the maximum limits are clearly marked by a large initial sign and then small repeater signs at regular intervals on lamp posts and telegraph poles. The 30mph limit is different in that there are no repeater signs.

If you are in a built-up area and you cannot see a sign it is best to assume that it is a 30mph limit. This is confirmed if the lamp posts are no more than 200 yards apart.

The only speed limits that are not compulsory are the advisory ones on bends and motorways. They are there, however, for your guidance and safety and should be obeyed.

Drink and Drugs

The old saying of 'never drink and drive' has been with us for many years, and will continue to be with us for many more. Alcohol does not sharpen the senses, it dulls them – so leave it alone if you intend to ride. Even one pint of beer, or a single whisky, is detrimental to your mental and physical abilities.

When the law states 'drugs' it is obvious that it means hard drugs as taken by addicts, but it can also include normal everyday medicines. Beware before you drive; check the label, or ask the doctor or chemist if it is safe to drive or not.

Maintenance Requirements

Legal requirements for roadworthy machines:

Brakes – must be maintained in efficient working order.

Lights – all lights, including stop lamp and indicators, must be clean and wrking.

Tyres – must be maintained at their correct pressures, and tread depth must be least 1mm. There should be no cuts or bulges.

Mudguards – every motorcycle used on the road must be equipped with front and rear mudguards.

Petrol tank – must be made of metal; it is illegal to use a fibreglass tank on the road.

Rear footrests – if a pillion passenger is carried adequate footrests must be fitted.

Exhaust – every exhaust must have a silencer fitted and this must be kept in efficient working order.

Suspension – both front and rear suspension units must be in efficient working order.

Speedometer – every motorcycle over 100cc must have a working speedometer.

Steering – the steering system, head bearings, etc., must be maintained in efficient working order.

Highway Code

The Highway Code is not binding in law. It is a set of guidelines to make our roads safer, and covers every road user, including those on foot and with animals.

Whilst it is not legally binding, it is often used in evidence in a court of law – usually by the prosecution – and should always be followed.

GEAR CHANGING

The basic principle of the gearbox is to alter the rate at which the rear wheel is driven by the engine. In the same way that using a smaller cog (higher gear) on a bicycle rear wheel makes the bike go faster with the same effort, a motorcycle has a selection of gears for much the same purpose.

For every gear ratio the motorcycle will travel at a certain speed per 1000rpm (revs. per minute) engine speed. For example: the Kawasaki Z1000 Mk II, used in most of the photographs in this book, has the following approximate road speeds for each 1000rpm – 1st gear 5.5mph, 2nd gear 8mph, 3rd gear 10mph, 4th gear 12.5mph and 5th gear (top) 14mph. So at 4000rpm in top gear the Z1000 will be travelling at about 56mph, but at 4000rpm in 3rd gear it will only be doing in the region of 40mph.

The gearbox is also used when ascending hills. To maintain the same speed it is often necessary to use a lower gear and increase the engine speed. When descending hills a lower gear is often chosen to produce greater engine braking on the over-run (throttle closed).

The clutch is purely a means of engaging or disengaging the drive between the engine, gearbox and rear wheel.

Clutch Operation

The use of the clutch is an important factor in motorcycle control. Smooth clutch control from a standing start and during gear changes is the sign of an experienced rider. Machine appreciation starts with clutch control, as does rider comfort and pillion passenger comfort. Nobody likes to ride on the back of a bike that has a rider making snatchy gear changes.

Upward changes can nearly always be made smoothly because the higher ratio in the gearbox can cope with a slight drop in revs. It is the changes down the box that usually result in snatching. To avoid this annoying problem practise 'blipping' the throttle slightly during the change – at the point when the clutch is fully disengaged (lever pulled in). Downward changes require the revs. to be maintained to guarantee a smooth change.

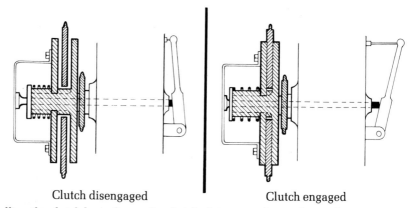

Clutch disengaged   Clutch engaged

Pulling the clutch lever forces the clutch plates apart by mechanical means. As the lever is gently released the plates come into contact (slipping) until the lever is fully out and the plates fully engaged.

Right Gear – Right Time

The advanced rider is always 'in the right gear at the right time', keeping the machine under power at all times, except when decelerating.

Certain factors influence a motorcycle, the main one during acceleration being the weight transfer to the rear. This has the effect of keeping the front end fairly light.

When the bike is under power the castor angle, a steering angle designed to make the front wheel travel straight, is also brought into action to aid stability.

Always being in the right gear at the right time has two main advantages, and they are both associated with passing through areas of danger (any crossroad, junction, town centre, village, etc.):

(a) you will be in a low enough gear to allow you to pass quickly through the danger area, once it has been ascertained that it is safe to do so, and . . .

(b) if necessary, the lower gear will give extra engine braking to stop before entering the danger area.

Gradients

It is obvious that a low gear is required to ascend or descend a steep hill, but a failing with many riders is that they leave the gear selection too late. This has the result of losing too many revs. on an incline, and having to go down two gears instead of one, or gaining too many revs. on a decline and having to brake too hard.

Descending steep winding hills requires a special technique. Engage a low gear early and rely on engine braking around the bends, using the brakes only on the short straight sections when the machine is upright. Modern brakes are not prone to fade and over-heating, but it can happen. Never rely on just the brakes.

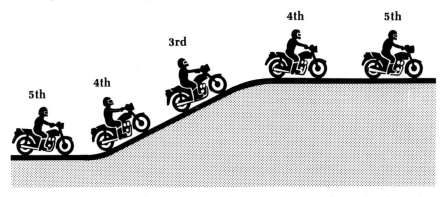

This diagram shows that downward gear changes are essential to maintain engine revs and road speed whilst ascending a hill. Make the changes early so that a minimum of speed and power are lost and ensure that you only need change down one gear at a time

Clutchless Changes

Modern gearboxes are so slick and smooth that it is very often possible to make gear changes without the use of the clutch. Most bikes will allow upward changes, but only one or two will allow the occasional downward change.

Upward changes are usually very smooth, and only require closing the throttle slightly during the change. Downward changes are nearly always snatchy because there is little chance of matching the revs.

Automatics

Some motorcycles are equipped with 'automatic transmission'. In actual fact they are not automatic in the same way as cars. They have two-speed manual boxes with centrifugal type automatic clutches. The two main models in Britain are the Hondamatic 400 and the Moto Guzzi V-1000 Convert.

The Hondamatic 400

ACCELERATION

Use of the Throttle

Smooth operation of the throttle goes hand in hand with smooth clutch control and machine appreciation. Harsh acceleration can cause wheelspin or wheelies; great for posers and fly boys, but bad for professional and caring motorcyclists, and bad for the general image of motorcycling.

Excessive use of the throttle, when not absolutely necessary, is also very expensive. The cost of fuel is always rising, so the less you open the throttle the better for your pocket.

Sitting at traffic lights or another hold-up, can also be expensive if you continually 'blip' the throttle. It can add 20 per cent or more to your fuel bill. The professional approach is to select neutral, leave the clutch lever alone and allow the engine to tick over.

Quick Action Twistgrip

Whilst quick action twistgrips are ideal for racing and fast road use, they can be awkward to handle in heavy traffic situations. A very small throttle opening develops a lot of engine revs., and makes smooth throttle control a very fine art.

Acceleration Sense

Acceleration sense is defined as the ability to alter the speed of the vehicle by the use of the throttle alone, and without touching the brakes.

The average rider uses acceleration sense frequently without really knowing it. Easing off the throttle in order to maintain an equal distance behind another vehicle, and then slightly adjusting the throttle to remain there, is acceleration sense.

It is the basis of fuel conservation and the result of perfect throttle control. It also helps to improve the motorcyclist's image. Nobody likes the rider who accelerates hard away from traffic lights and screeches to a halt at the next set of lights. The traffic overtakes him as the lights change, he accelerates past them, brakes at the next set of lights, and so on. This results in a waste of fuel, tyre rubber, brake pads, clutch material, etc., and a very bad image.

The advanced rider should control the throttle carefully in an attempt to pass the traffic lights as they turn to green. Racing and braking is expensive.

During overtaking the throttle should be controlled so that you arrive in the correct position on the road (see Chapter 11) to pass the other vehicle without the need for braking. Advanced observation (see Chapter 10) will show the need for acceleration sense and allow the rider to control his speed on entry to a danger area, and eliminate late panic braking.

Under acceleration the weight is transferred towards the rear, causing the back end to 'sit down' and the front become light. This is a very stable situation, and brings the bike's castor angle into play – an angle designed to maintain straight line running and self-centring

Fast Starts

Wheel spinning and wheelies are for the posers, they reflect a bad image if practised by the road user.

Wheel spinning can be prevented by slipping the clutch rather than just 'dropping it', whilst wheelies can be avoided by leaning well forward to keep your weight over the front wheel.

Rev. Counter

A rev. counter is a mechanical device which is controlled by a cable. The cable runs from the engine, usually from a camshaft take-off point, and turns the rev. counter in the same way as a speedometer. A tachometer is an electrical rev. counter that counts the engine's electrical ignition impulses.

It doesn't really matter which is fitted to your machine as they both serve the same purpose. They indicate the engine speed and have red sections to warn you when the engine is being over-revved, and stressed unnecessarily.

Make good use of the rev. counter during gear changing, especially when using the bike's maximum performance. With experience, a glance at the rev. counter will inform you how many gears to change down to maintain the same speed on a hill, or to get the quickest possible overtaking speed.

Know your machine. Go out for a ride and learn speeds against revs., so that you know exactly what limits you are riding within at any given time in any gear.

Maximum machine performance is gained by changing gear at the peak torque revs. (quoted in the bike's handbook). Performance drops off after this point.

A smooth multi-cylinder bike usually reaches its peak power at or near the red line, but a single cylinder bike often reaches its peak power point some 2000 or 3000rpm below the red line.

Get to know your bike and its power characteristics so that you can get the most out of it.

BRAKING

Today's motorcycles are equipped with either drum brakes, disc brakes or a combination of the two. When both are used the drum brake is always at the rear, being complemented by the more powerful single or twin disc arrangement at the front.

Drum brakes are cable or rod operated, and work on the principles of leverage. As the lever is pulled, or the pedal depressed, the cable or rod turns a cam which pushes the brake shoes out, and into contact with the drum.

Drum brakes are usually found on small capacity machines, or at the rear on larger machines if both drum and disc brakes are used

Most disc brakes are hydraulically operated, in much the same way as on cars. The principle of hydraulic operation is that the fluid cannot be compressed, so any force applied by a lever or pedal, via a small piston, is immediately transferred to the other end of the hose containing it. This force pushes the pads into contact with the disc(s).

1 A single disc at the front is adequate for lightweight motorcycles up to about 400cc

2 Heavy application of a rear disc brake can cause the back wheel to lock and skid

3 Powerful or heavy machines require twin disc at the front for maximum braking performance

There has been a lot of controversy over the years as regards the braking efficiency of discs in wet weather. Nearly every Japanese motorcycle was suffering from a long delay between the application of the brakes and the pads actually taking effect. In much the same way as a tyre rides on a cushion of water when aquaplaning so the disc pads were riding on a cushion of water between them and the discs.

The Italians never had the same problems. They use cast iron discs, which only cause a minimal delay, but do go rusty. Whilst this very fine superficial coat of rust disappears after

37

the first application of the brakes, the Japanese considered it bad for their cosmetic image.

Those who have bikes that suffer from a delay must allow for it in bad weather. This means braking early at all times.

The problem is slowly, but surely, disappearing. With Kawasaki leading the way the Japanese manufacturers are now using sintered metal pads. They have virtually done away with wet delay, but have reduced the dry braking efficiency very slightly. Bikes fitted with sintered pads have a braking efficiency which never varies, wet or dry.

If this bike wasn't fitted with stabilisers, for tyre testing purposes, the rider would not be able to stop with such confidence on the flooded surface. The tyres are aquaplaning on top of the water surface

Rules for Braking

(a) The brakes should only be applied when the motorcycle is upright and travelling in a straight line. Make full use of the gearbox for engine braking, as well as both the front and rear brakes.

Good forward observation is essential to ensure correct braking.

(b) The continued forward observation will also warn you of the condition of the road surface. Try to find a coarse, dry and firm section of road for heavy braking.

It should be obvious that if the road surface is loose or slippery you should ease off and vary the pressure.

(c) As explained in the chapter on gear changing, you should only brake on the straight sections when descending a steep winding hill, and use the gearbox and engine braking around the bends.

(d) The basis of good braking is to avoid using the front brake when the bike is leaning over, when turning, or when on wet, icy, loose, or highly polished surfaces, or when the surface is covered with leaves.

Influence on Machine

It is important that the rider fully understands the influence of braking on the motorcycle. Heavy application of the front brake has the effect of transferring all the weight forward on to the front wheel, sometimes completely compressing the forks. A heavy application of the rear brake alone only sends a small weight transfer forward.

The combination of both brakes not only transfers the weight forward but also makes the rear end very light. It is for this reason that the rear wheel is very easily locked, because of its lack of contact with the road, and why, on some machines, it is possible to actually lift the rear wheel under panic braking.

Whilst the machine is upright the effect of the weight transfer makes the front tyre grip the road for effective braking. If the machine is leaning over, as when negotiating a bend, the weight transfer has the effect of trying to push the tyre outwards, and it is then very easy to 'lose' the front end. In bends, therefore, if braking is necessary it should be via a light application of the rear brake or, depending on your experience and machine knowledge, an extremely light touch of the front brake.

In an emergency it may be desirable to apply the front brake hard in a bend and actually drop the bike, but this is a last ditch attempt to save hitting something very hard and immoveable.

Braking Percentages

Assuming that the road surface is coarse, firm and dry, you should aim to divide your braking so that it gives 75 per cent front and 25 per cent rear, making sure that neither wheel is allowed to lock and skid. Aim to keep the wheels just turning at a point just before locking. Remember: a skidding tyre is not a good method of braking.

During wet weather, or when the road surface is loose or slippery, amend your braking percentages so that they are split evenly: 50 per cent front and 50 per cent rear.

Brake Test

During the initial few hundred yards of your journey you should do a running brake test, just to make sure that everything is okay. Choose a straight quiet road and apply both brakes, one at a time, carefully and firmly.

During servicing and cleaning it is essential that greases, etc. are kept away from discs and pads, and water should be kept away from brake drums. Never use a hose pipe to spray a drum brake, it could fill with water and make the brake useless.

CORNERING

Principles and Safety Factors

Every bend is different, whether it be because of traffic, weather, camber or road surface, and should be treated as such. Never take anything for granted, and never be tempted to negotiate a bend faster than a speed from which you can stop in the distance you can see to be clear. Even if you know the bend extremely well, having travelled it every day for many years, there can always be something totally unexpected halfway round, and if you're travelling too fast you will not be able to stop or alter line.

The following principles are designed to ensure maximum safety at all times:

(a) You should be on the right line on the approach to the bend.
(b) You should be travelling at exactly the right speed, remembering that you must be able to stop in the distance you can see to be clear.
(c) Having decided on the right speed you should select the appropriate gear.
(d) You should be able to maintain the chosen speed whilst negotiating the bend. Keep the bike under power all the time,

but remember: never accelerate into a bend – only out of one.

If all the above principles are applied the following three safety factors will be evident as you leave the bend:

(a) You will be on the nearside of the road – approximately 4ft from the kerb;

(b) You will have no problem remaining there; and ...

(c) You will be able to stop safely in the distance you can see to be clear.

Once again the importance of advanced observation must be stressed. Without it the first of the four principles, correct positioning, will be impossible, and that will throw everything else out.

Technique

It is hoped that readers of this book will already have some experience of riding motorcycles, and will therefore know that in order to negotiate a corner or bend it is essential that the bike is leaning over. Trying to turn the handlebars, or negotiate a bend upright, at too high a speed will result in the rider being thrown off.

Only when travelling very slowly is it possible to manoeuvre the bike by turning the 'bars; at all other speeds (above walking pace) it is necessary to bank it over: to the left for a lefthand bend, and to the right for a righthand bend. The higher the speed the greater the angle of lean required.

The maximum angle of lean is dictated by several points: the skill of the rider, his confidence, the grip of the tyres, the road surface, weather conditions, road camber and items on the machine such as footrests, stands, exhaust clamp bolts, etc.

The centrifugal force created by leaning has the effect of forcing the tyre into contact with the road surface, unlike a car, where the force tends to lift the inside wheels and cause the outside wheels to slide.

Road Camber

The normal case is that lefthand bends can be taken slightly quicker than righthand bends, the reason being the slight camber on most roads which slopes gently from the centre of the road to the nearside kerbs.

Some roads have a greater camber than others, and some have a complete one-way camber or banking (a camber not from the centre but from one kerb to the other).

The effects of adverse camber tend to make the bike lean further than necessary for the speed. Extra care must, therefore, be taken in these circumstances, and the speed kept down. Bends with 'banking', or a continuous side to side camber, aid the motorcycle by allowing it to travel faster with less lean.

The effects of normal camber on a righthand bend can be minimised by following the correct line around the bend (see 'Righthand Bends'). This will have the bike moving away from the camber whilst it is actually on the bend.

Converging Verges

Certain bends on country roads, usually those with high hedges, can actually show you in advance what shape they are as you negotiate them. It is very disconcerting to suddenly find a bend tightening up, instead of opening out, and many a rider has been caught out.

Look ahead to the point where the two verges, or hedges, appear to meet, and pay particular attention to the inner one (the left hedge on a lefthand bend, and the right hedge on a righthand bend). The hedge will appear to be moving at this point. If it moves at the same speed all the time then the radius of the bend is constant. If the speed increases the bend is opening out, but if the speed decreases, or it appears to stop, the bend is tightening up.

This technique of 'converging verges', or 'the running hedge', is an excellent guide but it should never be used to ride quicker than a speed from which you can stop in the distance you can see to be clear.

Lefthand Bends

As soon as a lefthand bend is seen ahead the rider should take up a position near to the centre of the road, after taking the normal precautions of mirrors, shoulder check, and signal if necessary, to move off his original line. This position, out to the right, gives the maximum and earliest view into the bend, and is the start of increasing the radius of the bend for the highest possible safe speed.

Having taken up this correct position the rider should adjust his speed and gear to suit the bend as he sees it. Remember: better too

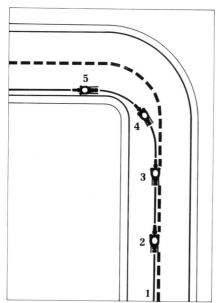

Lefthand bend: **1** correct line near centre of road; **2** select speed; **3** select correct gear; **4** peel off as the bend opens up; **5** leave the bend 3–4 ft from kerb. Keep the bike under power, but not accelerating, throughout the manoeuvre

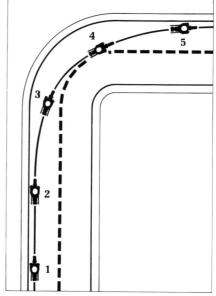

Righthand bend: **1** correct line near kerb; select speed; **2** select correct gear; **3** peel off as the bend opens up; **4** leave the bend near centre of road; **5** return to normal riding position

slow than too fast. Never coast or decelerate into a bend; a gear should be chosen that will allow the rider to keep the bike under power around the bend and then accelerate out of it.

Stay in this central position into the bend and look ahead for the road to straighten out. As soon as this is seen the rider should peel away from his line and leave the bend along the normal riding line, about 4ft from the kerb (see diagram on page 44).

This line is the ideal, not the essential. On a dry, firm and coarse surface it will be the fastest, safest line. The line should be modified as necessary on slippery or loose surfaces, or where the road is wet or icy.

Righthand Bends

On the approach to a righthand bend the rider should take up a position close to the lefthand side of the road, and then adjust speed and gear as per the lefthand bend. These precautions will ensure that the bike will be under power to negotiate the bend, and give the rider the maximum and earliest view into and around the bend.

In order to take the bend as quickly and safely as possible the radius must be increased. This is done by looking ahead and breaking away from the line around the outside of the bend in order to leave the bend near to the white line, or centre of the road, as the road straightens out. If there are no further bends the rider should return to the correct position on the road (see diagram).

In the same way as for lefthand bends, this line is the ideal, and must be modified if road or weather conditions dictate otherwise.

Emergency Procedure

Good observation will eliminate the need for emergency measures in nearly every case of taking a bend, but on the odd occasion something may be seen too late; spilt diesel oil, for example. Remember that closing the throttle, or gently braking, will tend to tighten the bike's line, and accelerating in the bend will widen the line.

OBSERVATION

A good clear view into the distance

Throughout the chapters in this book there is a definite emphasis on good observation, and with good reason. If you can't see and read exactly what is going on, both in front and behind, it will be impossible to plan the safest and fastest manoeuvre in any given situation.

Advanced motorcycling is based on planned riding. The approach to each bend, road junction, bridge, hill, roadworks, or anything that can be classed as a hazard, and everything can, is the critical part of good riding. A good rider never enters a danger zone whilst the danger exists, he uses good advanced observation to assess the situation ahead and adjust his line, speed and gear accordingly.

It is foolhardy to ride headlong into a known dangerous situation, but responsible and safety conscious to hold back and let the situation sort itself out. In a few cases it may be necessary to actually stop – never squeeze through a gap that may not exist when you're in the middle of it.

When riding in a queue of traffic it may not be possible to stop, but it could be necessary to lengthen the distance from the car in front to give you more time to assess things. Never be tempted to rush into any situation just because the vehicle in front does.

Road Surfaces

It would be a dream to ride through a town or county on a perfectly smooth and constant road surface, but in reality it is rarely possible to travel even the length of a fairly short road before encountering a change of surface, a repair or a pothole, not to mention the numerous manhole covers and miles of raised white road markings.

Changes in the road surface affect the tyre grip

When the wheels of a motorcycle pass from one surface to another the amount of grip afforded by the tyres alters; sometimes for the better, but mostly for the worse.

Materials such as metal and smooth white paint can be lethal to the motorcyclist, even in the dry, and proper advanced observation is essential to avoid mishaps. Look ahead and stay on the coarse sections of tarmac wherever possible. This rule is particularly important when the weather is wet or the bike is banked over.

Even during normal riding on a good surface it is good machine appreciation to stay away from potholes, manholes and ridges – there is no point stressing the tyres or suspension unnecessarily.

Weather Conditions

The obvious bad weather conditions, ice, snow, fog and rain, are all easily noticeable and easily adjusted to, but some are not so easily seen. Black ice is the major danger, and only your

47

appreciation of the ambient temperature and the occasional dab of the foot can confirm its presence.

High winds are another major hazard that are very dangerous to the motorcylist. During the major part of any ride the rider is normally aware of the winds, but after a spell of riding in a built-up area these winds can be forgotten. By applying good advanced observation, and mentally taking in everything you see, you will be made aware of any strong sidewinds in advance. Look for cyclists, cars, vans or other motorcyclists suddenly being moved across the road. Leaves, paper bags, coats and skirts being blown about are all indicative of strong winds.

Talk to yourself about everything you see – it will help you remember it and help you recall it quicker when needed.

Watch out for manhole covers, especially at high speeds

Vision and Speed

Speed dramatically affects the rider's vision. At low speeds the area automatically focused on is that just in front of the motorcycle. As speed increases your brain automatically makes your eyes focus further into the distance.

It is therefore necessary at low speeds to consciously make yourself look into the distance to pick up the information you will shortly be needing. At high speeds it is necessary to consciously look at the foreground, in order to maintain a watchful eye on road surface changes, loose gravel, manhole covers, potholes, etc.

Travelling at speed on a country lane that has high hedges the rider gets a greater impression of speed, and must concentrate even harder to look at the foreground.

Traffic Signs

Every traffic sign offers useful information to the advanced motorcyclist. Some are designed to be obeyed without question: traffic lights, stop, give away, etc., but most are there purely for guidance, and the good rider will make good use of them. Learn all the signs in the Highway Code (you should have done to pass your test anyway), but more important learn what they mean. For example: know the difference between 'double bend' and 'series of bends', and learn what the percentages now used to indicate how steep a hill is, actually mean, 20% = 1 in 5, 10% = 1 in 10, etc.

Look at direction indication signs, they will show you the layout of the junction or traffic island they refer to. Those on the approach to traffic islands and roundabouts will show which lane you require for your exit.

A selection of traffic signs: staggered junction; ahead only; 'one way' plate supplementing 'turn' signs; falling rocks

Direction sign at roundabout

Zones of Visibility

Whilst riding a motorcycle the road ahead is split into two categories; the bits you can see and the bits you can't – zones of visibility and invisibility. The bits you can't see are those that can hide dangers of various sorts.

Make full use of any low hedges, gaps in walls, hills, etc., to take sneak previews of parts you wouldn't normally see. Cars seemingly being driven across fields are actually on a road that could meet up with the road you are on.

The area in the middle of every junction or crossroads is the 'danger zone', or the place where most accidents occur. On the approach to it the advanced rider should adjust his position on the road, his speed and gear so that he can slow down or stop for other road users, or accelerate across the danger zone when sure that no other person will be endangered or put to any inconvenience.

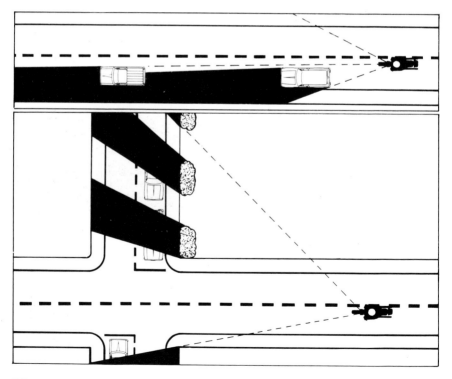

Country Roads

The main difference between town and country riding is the speed. Country riding is generally much quicker with a definite lack of 30, 40 or 50mph speed limits.

The general points of observation have been covered, but certain things only relate to country roads. Farms create many problems, such as animal droppings, mud near gates, slow moving tractors and unlit vehicles at night, to mention only a few.

During the autumn, fallen leaves are usually left on the roads, and these can be lethal to the motorcyclist, whether they are wet or dry.

In the winter, country roads are rarely cleared of snow and almost never salted or gritted. Some are even prone to flooding due to the lack of adequate drainage.

Even the spring and summer can hold unusual dangers, such as picnickers' cars badly parked, hikers and horses.

A word of warning – telegraph poles are usually a sign of the way the road bends, but beware, they can sometimes leave the line of the road and disappear across a field. Don't rely on them, unless the view from a hill confirms that they follow the road.

Slippery autumn leaves: lethal!

Clear view downhill

Telegraph poles can be deceptive

Town Riding

The art of observation when riding through towns and heavy traffic is very complex. There are many thousands of things all happening at the same time, any of which could constitute a hazard to the motorcyclist. It would be impossible to list every possibility, but the following is an indication of the sort of things to look for:

Buses pulling away from bus stops, stopping at bus stops, passengers alighting and walking out from behind the back or front. On old buses people congregating on the rear platform can indicate that the bus will shortly be stopping at a bus stop.

Traffic crossing the road ahead will indicate a busy road junction or set of traffic lights.

Brake lights a few cars ahead will mean that those just in front of you will soon be braking.

Traffic and road markings indicate that the junction ahead is with a more major road

Dogs are totally unpredictable, and even the laziest looking animal can suddenly make a dash across the road – give them plenty of room.

Children are as unpredictable as dogs, especially if there are some on both sides of the road, or if they are playing with a ball.

Watch for feet, legs or prams under and in front of parked vehicles. They will indicate someone starting to cross the road.

Exhaust fumes, someone in a driving seat, or the front wheels turning will indicate the possibility of a vehicle pulling out, or a door being opened.

Delivery vans (bread, milk, etc.) tend to stop anywhere, and even double park, in order to make their deliveries. Beware also of their doors being swung open.

Ice-cream vans are an obvious source of danger – when children have an ice-cream they tend to forget their Green Cross Code altogether.

Mirrors

In the so-called 'good old days' motorcycles were never fitted with rear view mirrors, mainly because there was little to overtake them, and also because the machine's vibration made them useless.

Today's heavy traffic conditions make mirrors essential, and most modern motorcycles are smooth enough to allow them to be fitted and used. Use the mirrors frequently so that you are fully aware of the changing situation behind. Don't be caught out.

Never rely solely on the mirrors, there are always blind-spots that are not covered. Having used the mirrors to assess the situation, before making a change of line, never make the move without making a shoulder check ('lifesaver'). You must ensure that it is perfectly safe to make a manoeuvre.

Under most circumstances the shoulder check is made over the right shoulder, but after overtaking, just before turning left or when leaving a roundabout, the check is made over the left shoulder.

Your own mirrors are not the only ones that can help you. If you look into lorry mirrors and car door mirrors as you approach and pass, you can see the driver's face and will know whether or not he has seen you.

The view in your mirror can tell you a lot

The car driver has probably seen you – note the eyes

POSITIONING

There are two main reasons for correct positioning. The first is to command your position on the road, and never to be put into a situation where other vehicles dictate where you ride. The second is to ensure that you eliminate as many blind-spots, or zones of invisibility, as possible in order to give the maximum view of the road ahead, and therefore maintain a level of maximum safety.

Whilst the normal riding position is 3-4ft from the kerb this is very flexible, and should be modified according to the conditions. Loose dirt, mud, greasy patches, etc., will all need a greater clearance.

The normal correct riding position relative to the kerb

Rule of the Road

Whilst it is generally known, and is mentioned in the Highway Code, that the 'rule of the road' in this country is to ride on the left except when overtaking, it is not illegal to ride on the right and there may be times when it is advisable. A flagrant piece of bad riding on the right will not result in a prosecution for 'riding on the right', although it could land one in court for dangerous driving.

If the road is clear, and there is good cause to do so, and no other road user is endangered or inconvenienced, then it is perfectly acceptable to ride on the 'wrong' side of the road; e.g. when passing parked vehicles, rubbish in the road, flooding, etc.

Vision

Changing your position on the road will also change your angle of view of the road ahead. In the same way, varying the distance behind the vehicle in front will also vary the angle of vision for maximum safety and knowledge. This is better explained by the accompanying diagrams.

Too close to heavy goods vehicle in front – view dangerously obstructed

Moving out gives a few feet of extra visibility

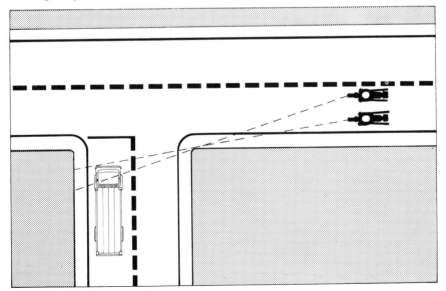

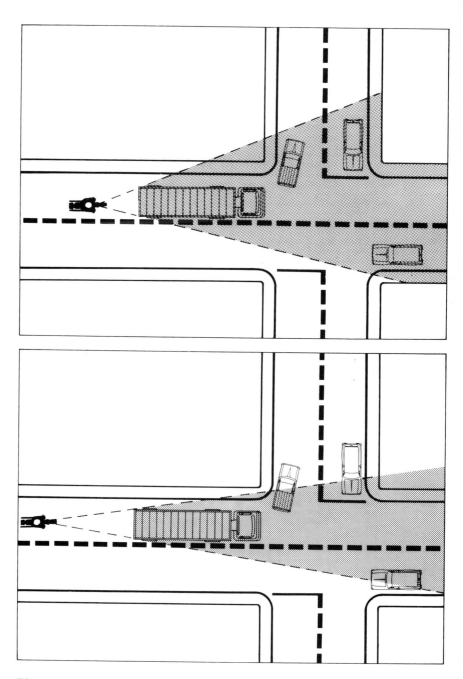

Moving about the road through a series of bends will give the rider views along both sides of the vehicles in front, especially if they are high sided vehicles. This is particularly useful when contemplating an overtaking manoeuvre, and this is also better explained by diagrams.

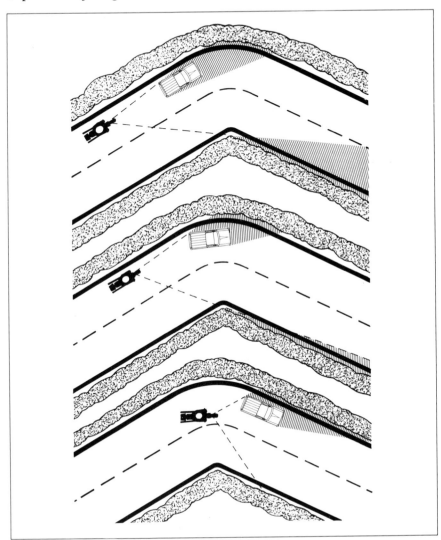

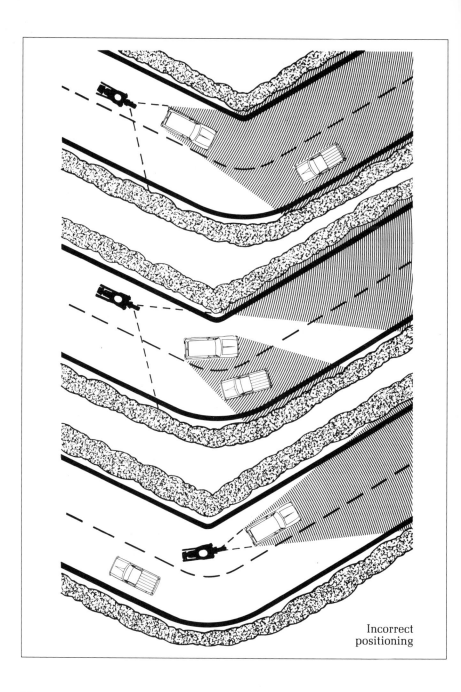

Incorrect
positioning

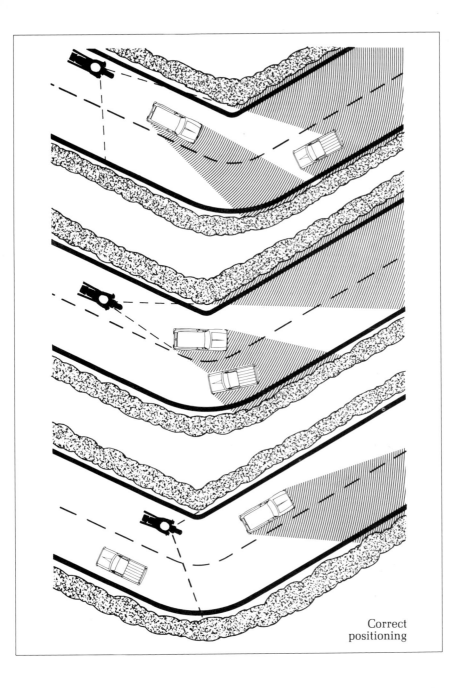

Correct
positioning

61

Lefthand Junctions

Many accidents occur at the point of a lefthand junction, and it must be said that the car driver, although he usually gets prosecuted, is not the only person at fault. If a motorcyclist approaches a lefthand junction near to the kerb he is at a very shallow angle to car drivers waiting in the junction, and easily hidden behind street furniture – trees, lamp-posts, etc.

For maximum safety and better vision, both into the junction by the rider and of the machine by the car driver, a position near to the centre of the road should be selected when passing a lefthand junction.

Passing a lefthand junction: the correct road position

Roundabouts

In traffic conditions the general rules for negotiating round-abouts are: (a) stay in lane: and (b) leave by the lane you enter, i.e. if you enter by the lefthand lane you should leave by the lefthand lane, and if you enter by the righthand lane you should leave by the righthand lane. Remember to give way to vehicles already on the roundabout and coming from your right.

The only time it is acceptable to 'straighten out' on a roundabout is when you are absolutely certain that no other road user will be endangered or inconvenienced.

Unfortunately, the majority of road users do not know that they are supposed to stay in lane around a roundabout, and the vulnerable two-wheeler must exercise great care to keep out of their way.

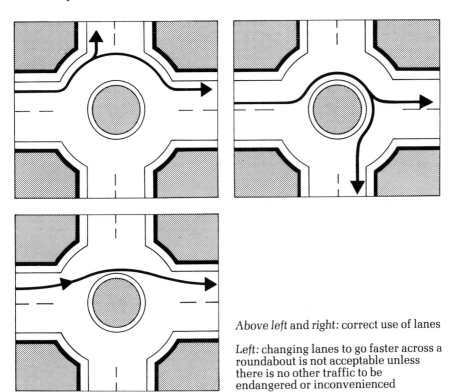

Above left and *right*: correct use of lanes

Left: changing lanes to go faster across a roundabout is not acceptable unless there is no other traffic to be endangered or inconvenienced

TOWN RIDING

Riding in town or city traffic requires an obviously different technique from riding on open roads. The number of dangers that are to be faced are virtually incalculable, and the majority can be lethal. The old saying of 'you need eyes in the back of your head' is a very apt one.

Traffic riding is both mentally and physically more tiring, with more concentration being necessary, more clutch work, more gear changing and more stopping and starting.

The greasy patch at the bus stop is clearly visible

Extra hazards occur at traffic lights and bus stops, where vehicles drop oil and grease. It can be slippery enough on a dry day, but when mixed with water it can be extremely dangerous.

Queues

The motorcycle is the perfect means of getting to the front of a queue of traffic, but it can also be the most dangerous.

If there is a wide enough gap between two lines of traffic it is acceptable, and legal, to ride slowly and carefully to the front, keeping a careful watch for pedestrians, opening doors, vehicles swapping lanes, etc. It is also acceptable to ride down the outside of two lines of traffic, again slowly and carefully keeping a good watch for hazards, but it is not acceptable, or legal, to pass on the wrong side of a keep left bollard as happens numerous times in city centres.

SPEED

It has been stressed that advanced riding is not an excuse to exceed speed limits and ride at dangerous break-neck speeds. Following the correct lines around bends will enable you to take the bend faster than the next man, but hopefully within the speed limits.

Remember the small motto 'safety fast', it is the one used by many police forces, and they have an excellent safety record.

Use of Speed

In Britain it is a sad fact that we are governed by numerous speed limits, including some maximum overall limits. A sad fact, but unfortunately a necessary one, not only for reasons of national economy (saving fuel) but also because very few people are capable of riding or driving at speed. The driving test in this country rarely has the vehicle being driven at over 30mph.

Speed limits should be obeyed, but all too often are not, so it is necessary to include a few notes for riding at high speeds:

(a) Practise everything that is mentioned in other sections of this book.

(b) Avoid tiredness – stop for a walk round and a cup of coffee if you feel drowsy.

(c) Never ride faster than a speed from which you can stop in the distance you can see to be clear.

(d) Never relax. Use all your powers of both skill and concentration all the time.

(e) Only ride fast when it is perfectly safe to do so and absolutely essential.

Use speed intelligently.

The Motorcycle

Cruising at the road's maximum speed limit can hold its problems because in the event of evasive action both braking and acceleration should be considered. If you are cruising at the bike's maximum speed you only have one choice – braking.

Always allow a minimum 10mph 'in hand'. In other words, if your bike's maximum speed is 70mph you should cruise at no more than 60mph, and so on.

NIGHT RIDING

Riding at night can produce many more hazards for the motor-cyclist than riding in daylight. Advanced observation is even more essential but considerably harder in most situations, and especially in towns. Objects and people are easily hidden in pools of darkness, and you have to rely on what you can see in your headlights, in other vehicle's headlights and in the glow from street lights.

It is common practice for most motorcyclists to ride with their headlights on all the time, even in daylight, so that they can be easily seen by other road users. This is essential in dark or dusk situations. Never rely on the bike's pilot or parking lamp – it will not help you to see or be seen.

Dipped/Main Beam

The general rule is to 'always use dipped beam', but on unlit roads it may be necessary to increase your seeing power and switch to main beam. The extra 5 or 10 watts of power, along a slightly higher beam, will let you pick out objects further in the distance.

Never use main beam in the face of oncoming traffic, and never use it when following other traffic – your glare could cause an accident. Try to use the other vehicle's lights, which may be better than yours, in order to see objects and the shape of the road ahead. Pay more attention to road signs. In the daylight you can usually see the hazard the sign refers to, at night you can't.

If you are dazzled by oncoming traffic don't be tempted to flash your lights back at them, it could cause an accident. Slow down and don't look at the bright glare. Try to concentrate on the road ahead, that you can see in your own headlight. Be prepared to actually stop if necessary.

If you are dazzled by following traffic, with the glare reflecting through your mirrors you should allow that vehicle to pass. Either slow down and call him past, or pull up and stop. Don't be tempted to push the mirrors out of the way.

Lefthand Bends

The pattern of a dipped beam is to throw light forward and to the left of the motorcycle, picking up the kerb a few yards ahead. On a lefthand bend at night the further into the bend you can see the better, and dipped beam, on certain bends, can be a distinct advantage. Main beam will very often pick up the hedgerows on the outside of the bend, not the nearside kerb, and can hide dangerous potholes and manholes in the darkness.

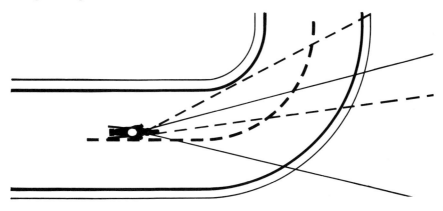

Street Lamps

It has already been stressed that you should never ride with anything less than dipped beam, even in areas lit by modern street lighting. Different types of lights, their differing heights, and their positioning in relation to the road can cause shadows or illusions that may lead you into a false sense of security. Don't take anything for granted – double check.

In many country towns and villages they still use the old forms of lighting, which are totally inadequate for today's conditions because they offer little light, and are too far apart to form a uniform glow. In these circumstances a rider is passing from pools of light into areas of darkness alternately for the length of the road. The dangers are obvious, so extra care and a lower speed are called for. Rely more on your headlight and less on the street lights.

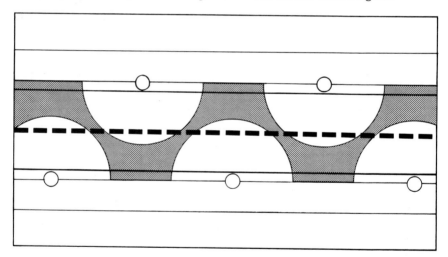

Visors

Always use a scratch-free visor, or goggles, at night, stopping frequently to clean it. A scratched or dirty visor will flare the light from oncoming vehicles and make it almost impossible to see – a highly dangerous situation.

In wet weather a scratched or dirty visor is made even more dangerous, in that water droplets collect in the scratches or on the dirt and flare the light even more. A clear, clean visor will aid the water to be blown off it whilst moving.

The picture above shows approaching headlights through a new and dry visor. Below is the effect when the visor is wet – the problem is made worse if there are several vehicles approaching

Never wipe your visor with your glove or overmitt – if you can't see properly try turning your head from side to side, the change in wind direction on the visor will push the water away. If this fails, raise the visor and stop to clean it at the first opportunity. Use plenty of water and a very soft cloth, allowing it to drip dry. Never just rub it, the dirt will scratch the surface.

Tinted Visors

Unfortunately, many riders use tinted visors at night, either because they are too lazy to change back to a clear one, or because they think it looks the 'in thing'. Whatever the reason, many come unstuck and several riders are killed every year because they simply couldn't see.

A tinted visor will only aid the darkness – not your vision.

Remember – SEE AND BE SEEN.

The clear visor *(left)* is to be preferred to the tinted one *(right)*, especially at night

ADVERSE WEATHER

There can only be one rule if it is essential to ride on a road that is anything but firm and dry – slow down and take extra care. In instances where four-wheel travel is dangerous it would be absolute lunacy to venture out on two wheels. Whilst you may be confident of completing the journey you have no control what-soever over the antics of others.

Rain

A very common occurrence in this country, but still one that very few people can properly adapt to. Instead of slowing down the majority of people actually go faster. Very few people increase the distance between themselves and the vehicle in front, and in the case of someone following a bike too close on a wet road it could prove fatal.

If you find a car too close behind, and this applies to all conditions, you must find a way of letting him past; slow down or stop. If you happen to fall off he will not be able to avoid running into you. It is worth allowing several vehicles to overtake in order to find a driver that will follow you at a sympathetic and safe distance.

Remember to dress for the weather – you must concentrate on your riding, not on the fact that your legs are wet or cold.

Fog

The best advice is 'stay at home', but if it is essential that you do venture out remember the golden rule – never ride faster than a speed from which you can stop in the distance you can see to be clear.

Give vehicles in front a lot of space and try to get rid of anyone following too close. Try and set up your piece of road ahead and behind.

Use dipped headlights because main beam will glare back off the 'surface' of fog and shorten the actual visible distance.

Avoid using your visor if possible. Fog is wet and will form a condensation layer on the front of the visor, and you won't be travelling fast enough for wind pressure to clear it. Without a visor in front of your eyes you can in fact see further, and may find that you will lead a queue of traffic, the drivers of which know you can see better than they can.

Snow

Normally when snow falls it turns to water on contact with the road, so riding conditions are basically the same as in the wet. The snow does, however, tend to collect on visors, jackets, windscreens, road signs, etc., making vision for yourself and others very restricted. Slow down and adjust to the conditions, taking extra care of other drivers.

Fresh packed snow will offer some grip to motorcycle tyres, but hard packed snow will be as slippery and lethal as ice.

Use the gearbox to slow down, the brakes will only cause the wheels to lock and slide.

Ice

The ice you can see is the best sort, you know it is there and can adjust your speed and riding technique accordingly. It is black ice, the sort you can't see, that causes the majority of accidents and incidents. On a very cold day, or after a very cold night, when the roads look wet take extra care – the water on the surface could be hiding a layer of ice.

Avoid banking over on icy or suspect surfaces wherever possible – keep the motorcycle as near vertical as you can.

Spray

Road spray has been around for many years, but has only been highlighted since the opening of the motorways, with the combination of their poor water clearing qualities and increase in heavy traffic.

The problems caused are twofold: excessive water, as in a heavy downpour; and poor visibility, as in fog, and riding techniques must be changed accordingly.

During the actual point of commitment, when overtaking a heavy vehicle, the rider is actually riding blind for one or two seconds, and that's a long time. At 30mph you cover 44 feet in one second, and at 60mph it is 88 feet. Two seconds in heavy spray could mean riding totally blind for a distance of 176ft, or nearly 60 yards. These distances emphasise the need for perfect and accurate observation of the road ahead just prior to commitment. There is no room for error.

MOTORWAYS

Whilst motorways have been a boon to Britain's transport industry, and cut hours off long journeys to certain parts of the country, they have created many problems for the motorcyclist. The spray, mentioned in the last chapter, the crosswinds, the draught from heavy vehicles, and more important – the lack of respect by other road users.

Many riders prefer not to use the motorways, feeling that they are dangerous and boring. A true rider prefers bends to monotony.

The regulations that apply are very simple, but essential to ensure safety. No stopping, no U-turns, no learners, no motorcycles under 50cc, etc., etc. The main ones are shown on signs at the entrance to the motorway, the remainder are common sense and are adequately covered in the Highway Code.

The speed limit signs at the entrance, e.g. 50, 60 or 70mph are obligatory, and must be obeyed, but speed limits shown on the overhead and central boards are advisory. You do not have to obey them, but remember: they are put there for a reason and for your safety. Ignoring them could result in a prosecution for dangerous driving, or a similar offence.

Make sure you have enough fuel for your journey, service areas can be few and far between.

Breakdowns and Emergencies

Should there be a need to stop because of a breakdown, puncture, etc., you should move quickly and safely on to the hard shoulder, making sure that all shoulder checks are made over the left shoulder. Use the hard shoulder to reduce speed and then stop as close into the grass verge as possible, keeping away from the carriageway. Never slow down on the carriageway and then pull sharply on to the shoulder to stop.

After the bike has been repaired, or the puncture mended, never rejoin the carriageway directly. Use the hard shoulder to move away and build up speed, before filtering safely back into the main traffic.

In the event of an emergency, where all the traffic in front of you is brought to a standstill, don't take your place at the back of a queue. You will be very vulnerable to following traffic that may not be able to stop, and a motorcyclist in a multiple pile-up doesn't stand a chance. Aim for a gap between two queues of traffic and try to work your way forward a few vehicles into a safe spot.

If the emergency ahead is an accident you will have to make a snap decision, whether to stop or take avoiding action. Remember that neither the carriageway nor the hard shoulder are very safe at the scene of an accident, and it may be necessary to ride on to the grass verge to keep out of the way.

Joining the Carriageway

The original concepts for the slip roads serving a motorway were that entrance slips would be downhill for increasing speed, and exit slips would be uphill to aid deceleration. Unfortunately, because of conditions applicable to many junctions these concepts have sometimes been reversed. But the principles remain.

The entrance slip road should be used to accelerate, and match your speed to that of traffic travelling along the nearside lane of the carriageway. Adjust your speed accordingly and filter on.

Travel in the nearside lane for a short while, in order to adjust to the new conditions, before moving into the centre or outside lanes for overtaking.

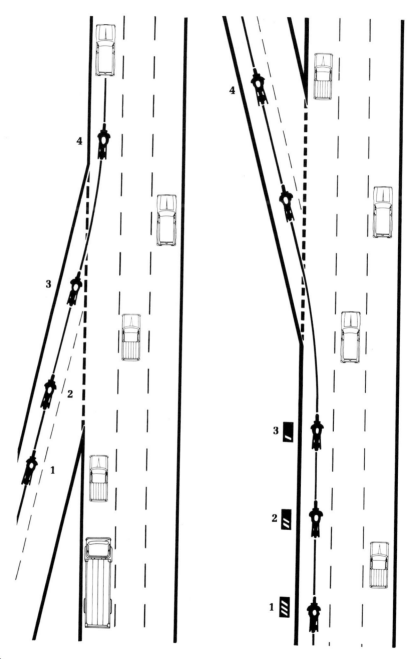

Leaving the Carriageway

One mile before your exit is an information sign, and your riding should be planned from this point. If the traffic is extremely heavy you should start moving to the nearside lane. A half mile further on is another warning, with a final one following that, just before the actual exit slip.

Your riding plan should aim to put you in the nearside lane no later than the 300 metre countdown board, just prior to the exit, at which time you should be travelling at the same speed as the rest of the traffic in that lane – no slowing down. Use the slip road itself to decrease your speed for the roundabout or junction ahead (see diagram on page 78).

Never overtake immediately prior to the exit slip and have to cut in sharply to leave the carriageway. It is very bad riding and not indicative of an advanced motorcylist.

If you miss your exit, for whatever reason, you must continue to the next one. You can then either re-adjust your route or go back to the desired exit.

Opposite page, left: joining the carriageway.
1 Adjust speed to that of traffic in nearside lane
2 Select gear and signal
3 Shoulder check; signal
4 Filter in and adjust speed to motorway traffic; cancel signal

Opposite page, right: leaving the carriageway.
1 Be in nearside lane before 300m countdown marker
2 Signal left at 200m countdown marker
3 Do not slow down until on exit slip road
4 Slow down and prepare for junction ahead

Overtaking

There are very few differences when overtaking on a motorway from when doing so on a dual carriageway; the main one is speed. Whilst an overall limit applies, and is the same as for dual carriageways, it is a fact that the traffic actually travels quicker.

Overtaking requires a lot of planning after thoroughly checking the road ahead and behind, bearing in mind that speeds can be very deceptive in wide open spaces.

Use the nearside lane, except when overtaking; it is not reserved for lorries and slow moving vehicles, as many people think. The centre and outside lanes of a three-lane carriageway are for overtaking only, although it is permissible to sit in a lane if passing a continuous line of traffic, and it is pointless returning to the left if there is a vehicle in the distance you intend to pass, providing you are not holding anyone else up.

Remember the problems that can be caused by spray, crosswinds, vehicle draughts, etc.

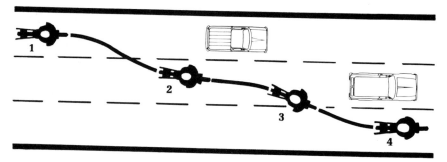

1 Use mirror, signal, and change to middle lane in plenty of time
2 Watch vehicle ahead carefully for any change of direction
3 The same procedure applies when moving from the middle to the outside lane
4 After overtaking manoeuvres are complete, move back to the middle and then to the nearside lane

OVERTAKING

A powerful motorcycle is just about the most perfect vehicle for carrying out the potentially dangerous manoeuvre of overtaking: a

While overtaking you may well be in the car driver's blind spot, but your headlamp will have given advance warning of your manoeuvre

manoeuvre that requires speed along with all the rider's powers of observation, concentration and skill.

Unlike most other manoeuvres, overtaking involves 'closing speeds', and this means that the rider must anticipate perfectly his exact time of overtaking. When you approach a road junction, or similar hazard, there is only your own speed to worry about, but when contemplating an overtaking manoeuvre with oncoming vehicles to take into account, your speed can be doubled. To anticipate your overtaking point you must react as though you are travelling towards a brick wall at your speed plus that of the oncoming vehicle. And that can be 120mph or more.

Timing is very important, and the advanced rider should aim to overtake at exactly the time the two vehicles open the gap after passing (see diagram below). This method will ensure that you cannot be overtaken just as you are committed to the manoeuvre, even though you will have made very careful checks in your mirrors, and a final right shoulder check ('lifesaver').

Apart from the obvious places never to overtake, all of which are mentioned in the Highway Code, you should never overtake on the approach to a garage or petrol station, no matter which side of the road it is on. Vehicles pull out without looking and many drop petrol and diesel oil on the road surface.

Overtaking through gap

Return to normal road position

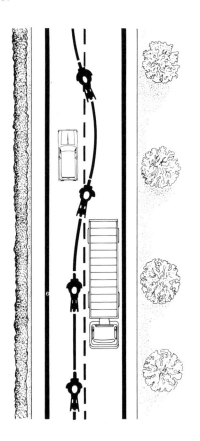

Overtake as gap opens up

Select correct gear just before
vehicles pass each other

Position for best view ahead

Bends

Believe it or not, one of the best places to overtake is on the exit from a righthand bend. The correct line for negotiating the bend not only gives you the perfect view past the vehicle ahead, but also has you leaving the bend in an overtaking position near to the centre of the road (see diagram below).

Lefthand bends can be the most dangerous place, unless there happens to be a perfect view across flat fields.

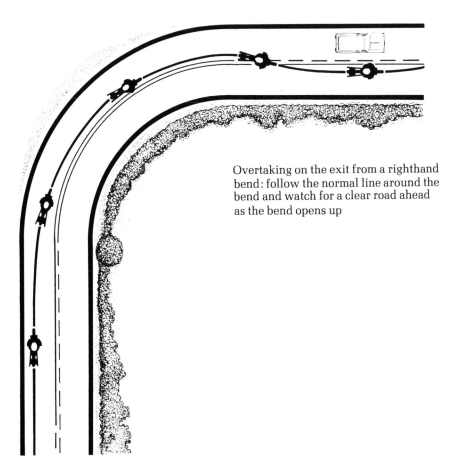

Overtaking on the exit from a righthand bend: follow the normal line around the bend and watch for a clear road ahead as the bend opens up

SIGNALS

The majority of today's motorcycles are equipped with flashing indicators, of a similar sort to those used on cars. Some even cancel themselves after a turn, or certain number of seconds, or certain distance travelled, but these are rare.

Unfortunately, these flashing indicators have made arm signals almost extinct, and the only ones seen are by riders of bikes that do not have the new luxury.

Arm signals are essential for safe riding in certain conditions. Strong sunlight can make flashing indicators virtually useless, especially the 6 volt system type, and other road users cannot tell whether they are on or not. If you have difficulty seeing other vehicles' flashers then it is safe to assume that they cannot see yours – use an arm signal as well.

If you are ever in doubt as to whether your signal has been seen, or are in doubt as to whether someone understands it or not, give an arm signal as a confirmation.

When slowing down to stop at the kerb give a slowing down signal – it will confirm your intention to stop.

Never call anyone across the road at a pedestrian (zebra) crossing, they may rely on your courtesy and be unaware of other traffic. On the approach to a crossing, if you intend to let people cross, give a slowing down signal. This signal will inform the people waiting to cross, the traffic following and the traffic approaching of your intention. The decision to cross should be left to the pedestrians.

As with direction indicators, stoplamps can be difficult to see at times, and are also prone to failure without being noticed. A slowing down signal whenever possible will aid your safety, and keep other drivers happy.

Arm Signals

In order to maintain perfect control of your motorcycle you should endeavour to make all arm signals short and positive. The Highway Code shows that arm signals are made from the shoulder with a straight arm, but this has your hands off the 'bars too long. The quickest, and shortest method for arm signals is to flick your arm, bent at the elbow, out from the waist (see photos). Maintain the signal for a count of approximately three seconds, before flicking your arm back to the handlebars.

Above left: turning right;
above right: turning left;
below left: slowing down

Flashers

Whilst it has become general practice to flash headlights to say 'thank you' or 'after you' it must be said that this is a very dangerous practice. If more than one person acts on a signal of this type an accident could occur. Never use the headlight in this manner and never trust a signal given by someone else.

The true meaning of a flashed headlight is the same as the sounding of the horn – it is warning of your presence or approach. It should be used on unlit roads at night, where a flash from dipped to main beam will warn others of your presence. On a fast road, where it is impossible to hear a horn, a flash of the headlight will warn vehicles in front of your presence and assist them in judging your speed.

Don't use the headlight aggressively, i.e. continually flashing someone to move out of the way on a motorway – it will only annoy them and make them stay where they are. One flash, of about three seconds, should be given whilst you are still quite a long way behind.

Too long a flash can dazzle other drivers. The use of main beam all the time is even more dangerous

Thank You

There is only one correct way to say 'thank you', and that is to raise your left arm, palm facing forwards, to your chest (see photo right). Never flash your lights or wave. If you don't have time to raise your arm, a quick nod of the head should be given.

Hazard Warning Lamps

A few motorcycles are fitted with a hazard warning system. A switch flashes all four indicators at the same time. They tend to be more of a gimmick on a bike than on a car, but can be useful in the event of a breakdown or accident – especially at night – to warn others of your obstruction.

Horn

The horn is a device for warning other road users of your presence, it is not a means of aggression, or a means of calling to your friends.

It should be used when another road user may not have seen you, or just prior to overtaking. It is of particular use when about to overtake a cyclist, who probably does not know what's going on behind him, but it must be remembered to signal early. If it is too late it may take the cyclist by surprise and cause him to wobble or fall off.

Opposite page, left: the correct points at which to sound the horn are indicated by the solid circles
Right: the right and wrong use of the horn when overtaking a car and when approaching a road junction

Horn button

If all the safety factors, mentioned in other chapters, are taken there should be little need to use the horn.

Remember: it is illegal to use the horn in a built-up area between 11.30pm and 7.00am, but in an emergency it may be necessary to break the law in the interests of safety.

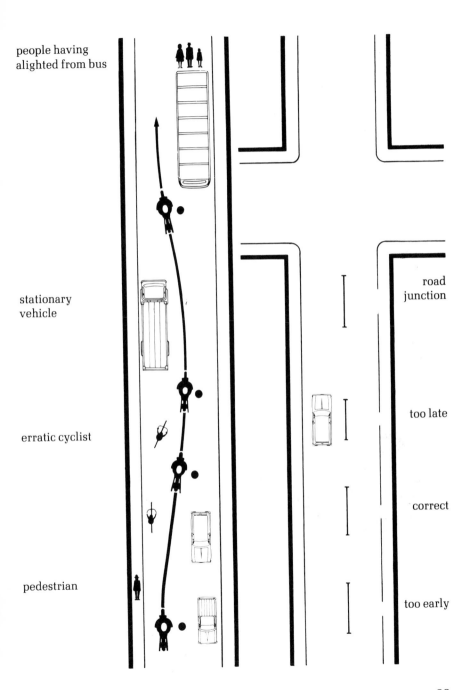

people having
alighted from bus

road
junction

stationary
vehicle

too late

erratic cyclist

correct

pedestrian

too early

ACCIDENTS

By following the advice given in the previous chapters of this book you should never find yourself in a situation when an accident is inevitable. But, having said that, anything is possible, and it is necessary to know what to do in the event of an accident being unavoidable.

Whilst there may not be time to stop or take avoiding action there could still be time (only fractions of a second are needed) to turn your thoughts and actions to self-preservation.

Try to put all the following principles into operation if you cannot avoid hitting an immovable object – such as a car:

(1) Reduce speed as much as possible.
(2) Hit the object square on – avoid glancing blows.
(3) Remove thumbs from around 'bars – lay hands flat across grips and levers.
(4) Slide balls of feet on to footrests.
(5) If you realise you are airborne look for your feet – it will help you curl up into a ball.

These principles will not stop you being injured, but could avoid serious injuries or death.

The motorcyclist is much more vulnerable than the car driver in an accident

First Aid

If you arrive at the scene of an accident what should you do? Unless you have been properly trained in first aid the answer is 'very little'. It is possible to do more harm than good if you start to help people when you don't know what you are doing.

In some circumstances it is absolutely essential that you take some action. If the victim is in peril of his or her life, e.g. their car is on fire, or they are lying on the carriageway of a motorway, they must be moved as quickly, but as gently, as possible.

The other time when action is essential is if it is obvious that the victim is not breathing. Clear the mouth of any obstructions, false teeth, sweets, etc., and apply mouth-to-mouth resuscitation.

Always call the Police and an ambulance if someone is injured, and consider the need for the Fire Brigade in the event of a fire or trapped person. If you send someone to dial 999 always send at least two people, just to make sure someone makes the call.

TRAIL RIDING

Off-road riding is a popular pastime with many motorcyclists, and involves the dual-purpose trail bikes – motorcycles that are at home on both roads and the dirt. They are designed with greater ground clearance, greater clearance between tyres and mudguards, higher footrests, longer suspension travel and 'knobbly' tyres.

It is an excellent hobby and can be a very good way of keeping fit. A tough ride requires a lot of physical strength and endurance.

When riding in sand the bike should be kept under power to keep the front end light and avoid it digging in

Never ride into water without knowing its depth or what's on the bottom. Keep the engine revving all the time and dry the brakes after leaving

In order to negotiate a log, or similar object, it is necessary to lean on the bars to depress the front forks, then pull back and blip the throttle in order to lift the front wheel. As the rear wheel touches the obstruction it will climb it as the front end descends

Power is applied on the approach to the slope and maintained until the front end clears the rise. As the bike starts to climb the slope the rider should stand up and lean slightly forwards, keeping the handlebars towards the chest and the weight directly down over the rear wheel spindle

Avoid using the brakes when descending a steep slope. Select a low gear and keep your weight towards the rear (over the rear wheel spindle) as the bike moves over the edge and down

Where to Go

Whilst the number of 'trails', or green lanes, is decreasing slowly, especially because of problems with vehicular traffic, there are still many miles of nice rough tracks that can be explored by motorcycle. They provide a challenge to the demanding rider, especially when the way is made difficult by mud, sand, fallen trees, water, rocks, steep hills, etc.

If you are not sure of which 'green lanes' you can ride along in your area, you should contact either the local Police or the local motorcycle club:

Don't forget – take litter home and respect the countryside.

Courtesy

The reason that many green lanes are being closed to vehicular traffic is that other groups, hikers and horse riders, complain about the conduct of car drivers and, more important, motorcyclists. Inconsiderate riders on noisy motorcycles create many problems for the considerate, and comparatively quiet, discerning riders.

Slow down on the approach to hikers, picnickers, farmers and horse riders; give them a wide berth and a friendly wave. If you have time you could even stop and have a friendly chat, it does the world of good.

Preparation

Some green lanes can take you miles away from civilisation, so it is essential that certain preparations are made. Top up the petrol tank before leaving, and know how far you can go on reserve. Carry a spare inner tube and valve inners, or a can of Finilec (tyre sealant/inflater). Make sure the bike's toolkit is complete and that there are enough spanners, etc. for all the nuts and bolts on the bike.

Most important preparation job, especially if it's a long ride, is to ensure that regular and proper maintenance is carried out. This will reduce the risk of a breakdown miles from anywhere.

Be sure before you go – it will be too late once under way.

Clothing

Trail riding is warm work and it is usual to wear lightweight but protective clothing. Ideally you should wear a jumper with padded elbows and shoulders, and jeans with padding to the knees and hips, in a similar style to those worn by motocross riders. Spills are frequent, and you need a bit of protection.

It's the boots, helmets and gloves that are the really important articles of clothing.

The boots should be near knee length and offer a lot of ankle support. The best sole is of the 'Commando' type, to give better grip in awkward situations.

The open faced style helmet is the type normally used – it keeps the rider cooler and allows goggles to be worn. A visor on a full face helmet will soon steam up when the going gets hot.

Hands are frequently whipped and bashed by bushes and trees, and it can be very painful. Choose gloves that have padded fingers and knuckles.

Tyres

The semi-knobbly tyres used on trail bikes are a compromise for a dual purpose. The knobbles are not big enough, or widely enough spaced, to be very good in the dirt, and likewise they are too big to be very good on the road. Whilst being under-tyred on the rough is no major problem, it can be dangerous on the road. Cornering is not as good as with road tyres, and road holding (grip) is very bad in the wet.

On the dirt it is better to lower the tyre pressures to about 15psi, for better grip, but remember that this would be illegal on the road (even crossing a road from one track to another), and it is essential to have some means of blowing them back up at the end of the trail.

Braking

Stopping, or even slowing down, can often be a problem. Using the brakes on loose, muddy or sloping surfaces can cause a total lack of control, or even a spill. Make full use of the lower gears and deceleration.

Keep the front wheel straight when braking on most dirt surfaces – if the wheel is turned, or the bike leaning over, the chances are it will 'break away' and slide.

Trail tyre

TOURING

Preparation

Whether the distance you intend to travel is a few hundred or several thousand miles it is essential that you are fully prepared before you leave. Service the motorcycle from the front to the back, carry enough tools (adjustables take up less room than several kinds), carry a few essential spares, and most important: make sure you have enough warm and dry clothing. Don't be uncomfortable on a long journey, you'll regret it.

Plan your trip in advance by checking your route on a map. Tot up the mileages and work out, at an average speed of about 40mph (unless it is all motorway), how long it's going to take, add on meal stops. Leave at your planned time – if you leave late you may try to make up for lost time, and your professionalism may suffer.

Write out your basic route (see photo), keeping it very simple, towns and road numbers, and tape it, in a plastic bag, on to your tank or tank bag.

A written route plan helps greatly

With today's modern road sign system the art of reading a map is slowly dying, but it is important to buy the best map you can afford. Buy one that gives the maximum information in the clearest style. If you are not sure what the various symbols and road colourings mean check the key on the map. You may need your map to help with any necessary deviations from your planned route, so don't leave it at home.

Luggage

Regular and serious touring riders will probably have panniers and a top box fitted to their bike, and the only extra may be a tank bag. Riders that like naked bikes most of the time will turn to the soft luggage, bags that can be strapped to the bike (see Accessories – page 105).

Don't be tempted to carry a bag, light or heavy, on your back; it will soon cause discomfort and distract your concentration.

750cc machine with top box and panniers

Soft luggage

Cameras

The best place to carry a camera, unless it is a pocket type, is in a tank top bag, and on a layer of soft clothing. Don't put it anywhere it can be affected by vibration.

Pillion Passengers

Many accidents have been caused by pillion passengers not acting correctly. They move about and cause the motorcycle to wobble, and don't always lean the right way in bends.

Instruct your passenger to lean slightly forward towards you at all times, and lean exactly with you, no more and no less, when you take bends. And never take a new passenger on a long journey without first having been for a few practice rides.

Fully laden and with pillion passenger: the back-bag is bad practice

Continental Touring

The main obvious difference in riding on the Continent is the fact that you ride on the right, not the left. This is not very difficult to adapt to, and is certainly easier on a bike than it is in a car. The secret is to take it slow at first and adapt to the environment; the problem is re-adapting to riding on the left on your return home.

Your preparations before you go should be even better than touring at home, and should include contacting either the embassy of the country you are visiting, or a travel agent. They will supply you with all the information you require, including traffic laws and signs, currency value and exchange, local customs, etc. Be prepared before you go and you will have more time to yourself when you get there.

Ferries

There is little to explain about cross-channel ferries because the details are all sent with your booking, the main point of this section is to warn you of the entrance and exit ramps to and from the ferry. The wet metal is very slippery and highly dangerous. Take your time and don't try to rush things.

ACCESSORIES

The addition of various accessories can make life easier for the serious motorcylist. There are many different accessories available, some are very good and are extremely useful, some are plain rubbish and are really sold as 'gimmicks'. Some are legal to fit but illegal to use, such as radar trap detectors.

Don't spoil the overall appearance of your bike by buying what your local shop just happens to have in stock, no matter what their recommendation is, it is probably not exactly what you want, and is more than likely more expensive than you were hoping to pay. Shop around, read the small ads. in the motorcycle press and visit shows if you can. Altering your bike, which is what adding accessories really is, should be given the same consideration as buying the bike itself.

Consider what the bike is to be used for most of the time, and start there. Many people own a big touring motorcycle fitted with a fairing, top box and glass fibre panniers, and for the biggest part of each year they use it to commute a few miles to and from work. For two weeks, during the summer holidays, it becomes what it is supposed to be – a long distance tourer. There is no problem with the fairing, that may be a necessity for many riders, but what about the top box and panniers? The chances are that most of the time they will be empty, or only carry an oversuit, a few extra tools and the rider's lunch. They become unnecessary and expensive accessories which can also affect the bike's handling qualities, especially when empty.

With a bit of forethought the sensible rider would buy a tank top bag to carry the oversuit, tools and lunch. It can be removed from the bike and carried as a case and, depending on its size, will hold much more. For the summer holidays a set of 'throw-over' luggage is more than adequate. In fact the complete combination of tank bag, tank panniers, saddle panniers and stuff bag will hold much more than a glass fibre top box and pannier arrangement.

105

And so it goes on. The horns fitted to many Japanese bikes are virtually useless and air horns should be considered. There is always room for improving the headlamp, etc., etc. Choose wisely, and within your own particular needs.

The following accessories are not necessarily recommended, bearing in mind individual needs, but they are representative of what's available on the market:

Sports fairings offer a certain amount of protection from the elements, but are basically designed for streamlining effects

Touring fairings offer full protection for hands and feet and are usually more square than sports types

Handlebar fairings only offer protection for the hands and upper body

Windscreens are ideal for the smaller machine, keeping the wind and rain off the rider's face and chest

Replacement seats can be fitted to create greater comfort on a long journey. This is a 'King and Queen' type

Fibre glass petrol tanks are illegal so these racing type covers are the next best thing

Many motorcycle horns are only just better than useless so the addition of air horns is a wise move

If you can't afford an alarm you could buy a chain and lock in order to secure your bike to an immovable object

Fibre glass panniers and top box are the permanent way to carry all your gear

Crash bars, when fitted front and rear, can help avoid damage to the machine and rider in a minor accident

Rear carriers offer an ideal place for securing oversuits and parcels with aero-elastics, and an excellent base for a stuffabag

Beat the thief and fit an immobilising alarm – especially if you leave the bike parked for long periods of time

Four-into-one exhaust systems not only tidy up the pipework, but some also claim to increase performance as well

MAINTENANCE

This final section is devoted to the maintenance required by your motorcycle to keep it in a sound roadworthy condition, but it can only be a very brief guide. There are many different bikes on the market, and many more different techniques with regard to servicing requirements.

If you intend to service and maintain your own bike it is essential to obtain the workshop manual that relates to it. If you only intend to carry out simple plug cleaning and gapping, oil changes and general elementary maintenance procedures this guide may be sufficient, but you will need to adapt these techniques to your own bike.

Check tyre pressures regularly and properly using an accurate gauge. Always check them when the tyres are cold to avoid false readings, and follow the recommendations of the tyre manufacturers

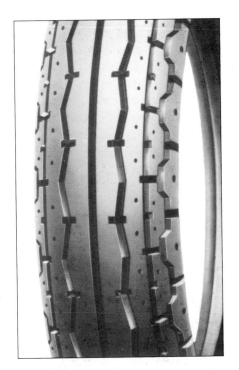

The minimum legal tread depth is 1mm but for safety's sake you should not let the depth get below 2-3mm before renewing the tyre. Check also for cuts and bulges, they are dangerous and illegal

Wheel spokes should be checked for tightness by tapping them with a screwdriver – they should all 'ping'. A dull note indicates a loose spoke that needs careful tightening

Wheel bearings are checked for play by pushing and pulling the wheel rims at opposite sides. Movement indicates a loose bearing. Some can be tightened, others require renewal

Drum brakes are adjusted at the cable as and when necessary to maintain optimum efficiency

Disc brakes shouldn't need adjusting, but the pads do need replacing when the pad material has worn down

Steering head bearings are checked for play by pushing and pulling the bottom of
the front fork legs. If movement is felt the top nut is slackened and the bearing
carefully and progressively tightened to take up the slack. Make sure the
handlebars can swing freely from lock to lock after adjustment

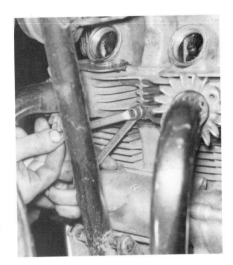

Cam chain adjustment varies from bike
to bike so it is essential to consult the
workshop manual

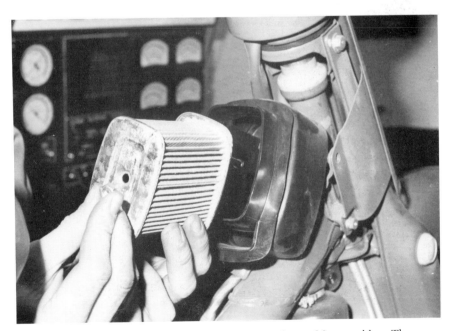

There are two main types of air filters; paper cartridge and foam rubber. The
paper type should be renewed when dirty, but the foam element filters can be
cleaned in a high flash-point solvent. Some filters are soaked in two-stroke oil
after cleaning, some aren't – check your handbook

Ignition timing is crucial for optimum performance and economy and is best checked using a strobe light. The contact breaker points back plate is usually moved to set the timing and line-up the marks on the flywheel and engine case – check the workshop manual for full details

118

Timing a two-stroke requires a dial gauge in order to check that the piston is exactly a certain distance before top dead centre (BTDC) when the timing marks are aligned

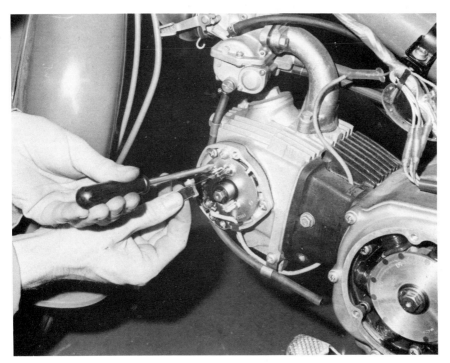

Contact breaker points should be cleaned with a points file or emery cloth and gapped according to your bike's handbook – usually 0.015in

Some bikes use shims for valve clearance adjustment, but the majority use tappets.
Valve clearances must be gapped correctly according to the bike's handbook

Rear drive chain tension is critical and should be adjusted to give approximately 0.75 to 1.25in of free play in the middle of the lower run

In order to prolong the life of the rear chain and its sprockets it should be regularly lubricated with a proprietary chain lube grease

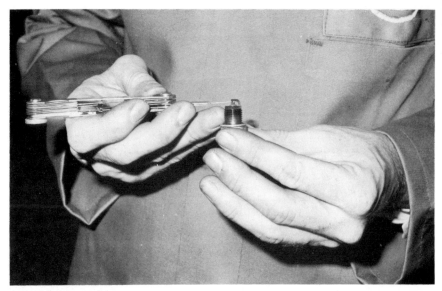

Spark plugs should be gapped at regular intervals. The condition of the plug indicates carburation settings; a whitish plug shows a weak mixture and a black plug indicates a rich one. The ideal colour is a light chocolate brown on the electrodes

Major clutch adjustments are made at the pushrod and vary from bike to bike – check your handbook

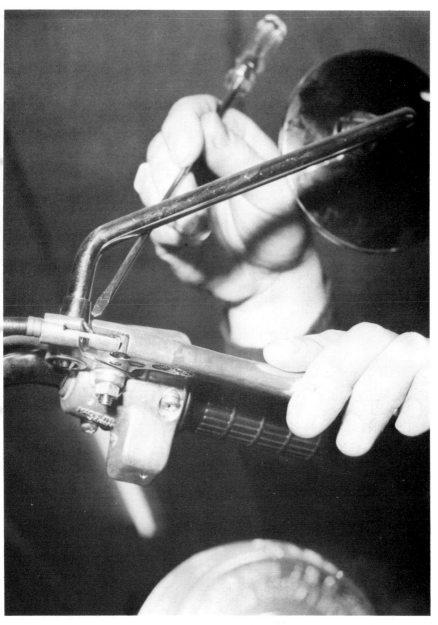

Minor adjustments are made at the clutch lever cable adjuster, and should allow for about 0.25in free movement at the end of the lever

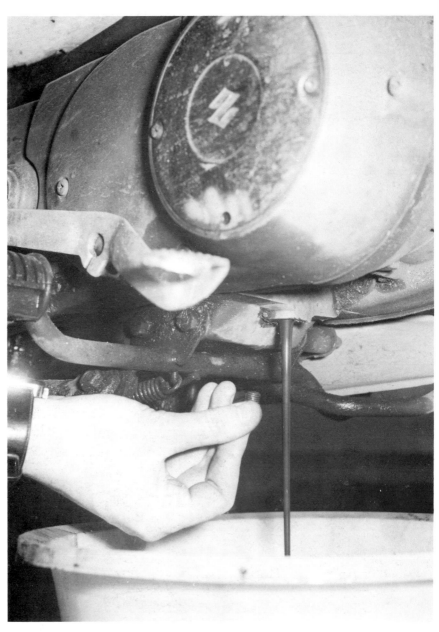

Oil is the life-blood of every engine and gearbox and should be changed at the recommended intervals – usually every 3,000 miles

The oil filter is usually changed every other oil change – an essential maintenance item

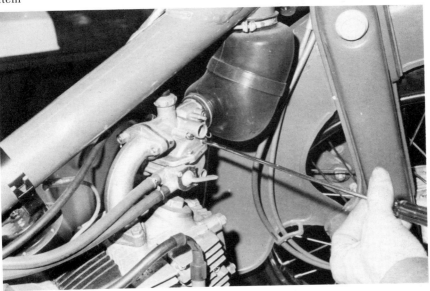

Single carbs are easy to set up, but twin and multiple units require balancing so that every carb produces exactly the same performance. This is done with either a vacuum gauge or by listening to the air intake noises with a stethoscope

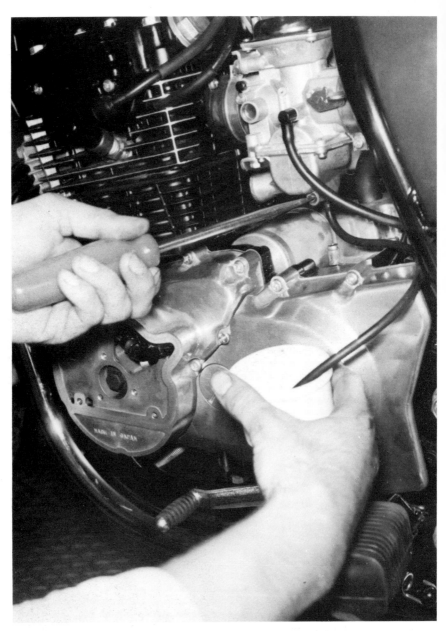

Sediment from the petrol collects in the carburettor float bowls and must be cleaned out, either by draining the bowls or completely removing them

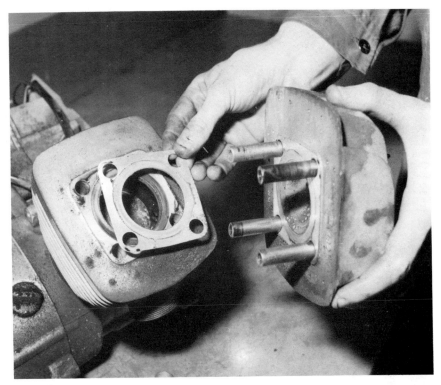

Two-stroke engines need fairly frequent decoking (the removal of carbon deposits from the combustion chambers). Both cylinder head . . .

. . . and the piston crown should be gently scraped with a piece of wood, not metal, to remove the deposits. Care should be taken not to scratch and damage the engine components

Picture credits